OXFORD

First
PICTURE
DICTIONARY

Illustrated by Val Biro

Compiled by Sheila Pemberton

OXFORD
UNIVERSITY PRESS

OXFORD
UNIVERSITY PRESS

Great Clarendon Street, Oxford OX2 6DP

Oxford University Press is a department of the University of Oxford.
It furthers the University's objective of excellence in research, scholarship,
and education by publishing worldwide in

Oxford New York

Auckland Bangkok Buenos Aires Cape Town Chennai
Dar es Salaam Delhi Hong Kong Istanbul Karachi Kolkata
Kuala Lumpur Madrid Melbourne Mexico City Mumbai Nairobi
São Paulo Shanghai Taipei Tokyo Toronto

Oxford is a registered trade mark of Oxford University Press
in the UK and in certain other countries

Text copyright © Oxford University Press 1994
Illustrations copyright © Val Biro 1994

Database right Oxford University Press (maker)

First published in 1994 as My Oxford Picture Word Book
This edition in 2004 as Oxford Picture Word Book
This edition in 2010 as Oxford First Picture Dictionary

British Library Cataloguing in Publication Data available

ISBN 978-0-19-911984-4

1 3 5 7 9 10 8 6 4 2

Printed in China

Introduction

This **Oxford First Picture Dictionary** is designed to give confidence and support to young readers and writers in using their early dictionary skills. Children can correct their spelling, and can check the way words are used. The text is illustrated by Val Biro, who is immensely popular with children, and his pictures will provide entertainment, fun, and also a useful key to understanding the meaning of words.

The word book is divided into three sections:

A-Z of first words
This section contains over 500 words in alphabetical order. The range of words chosen includes a helpful blend of nouns, verbs, and adjectives, which appear regularly when children write about their daily lives, interests, and pastimes. Each word is accompanied by a phrase and supported by a lively picture.

Words we write a lot
This is a list of words such as *for*, *with*, *into*, which children often refer to for spelling help. It is very useful in the early stages of writing.

Special picture section
These pages are bursting with colour and humour and show numerous scenes including a picnic in the park, a school sports day, going to the dentist, an adventure in space, and well-loved fairytale characters. The objects on each page are clearly labelled to show groups of words that children encounter every day.

Enjoy using the **Oxford First Picture Dictionary**. Hours of pleasure and discovery are packed into every page!

Contents

Aa

above
flying above the trees

accident
a car accident

ache
a tummy ache

airport
waiting at the airport

ambulance
going in an ambulance

animal
an animal picture

ankle
a swollen ankle

apple
an apple tree

arm
walking arm in arm

asleep
in bed asleep

audience
an audience cheering

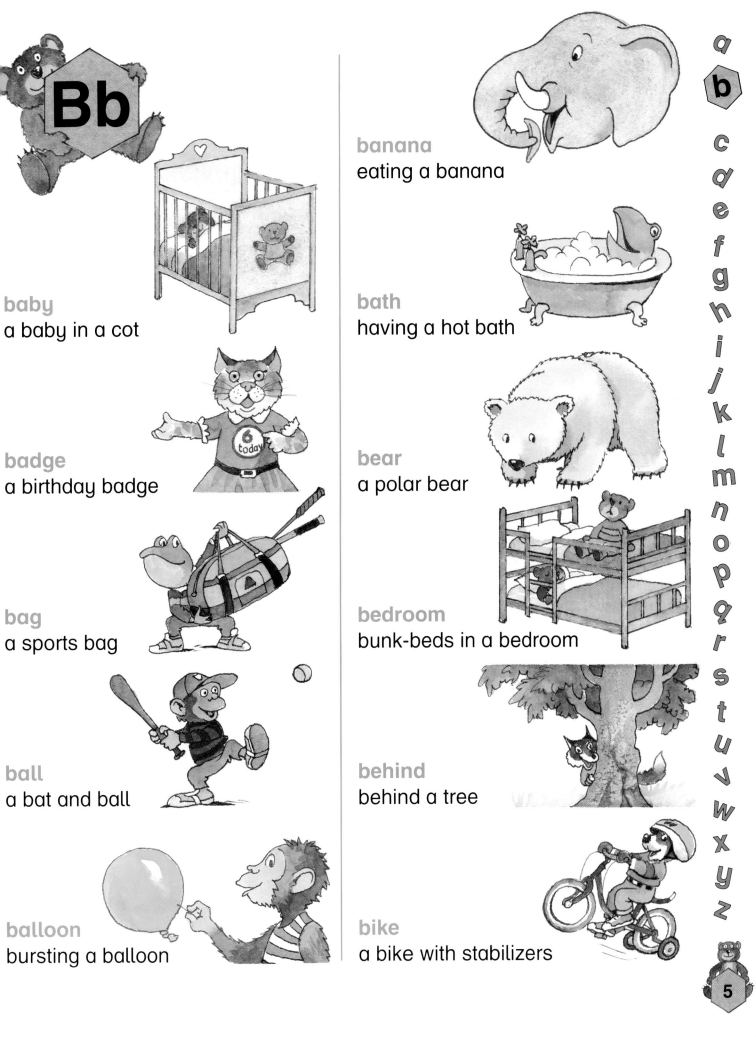

Bb

baby
a baby in a cot

badge
a birthday badge

bag
a sports bag

ball
a bat and ball

balloon
bursting a balloon

banana
eating a banana

bath
having a hot bath

bear
a polar bear

bedroom
bunk-beds in a bedroom

behind
behind a tree

bike
a bike with stabilizers

a b c d e f g h i j k l m n o p q r s t u v w x y z

5

bird
a bird in a nest

birthday
a birthday present

biscuit
a chocolate biscuit

boat
a motor boat

book
reading a book

bottle
a bottle of milk

box
a box of chocolates

boy
a little boy

bread
bread and butter

breakfast
breakfast on a tray

bridge
fishing from a bridge

brush
brush your hair

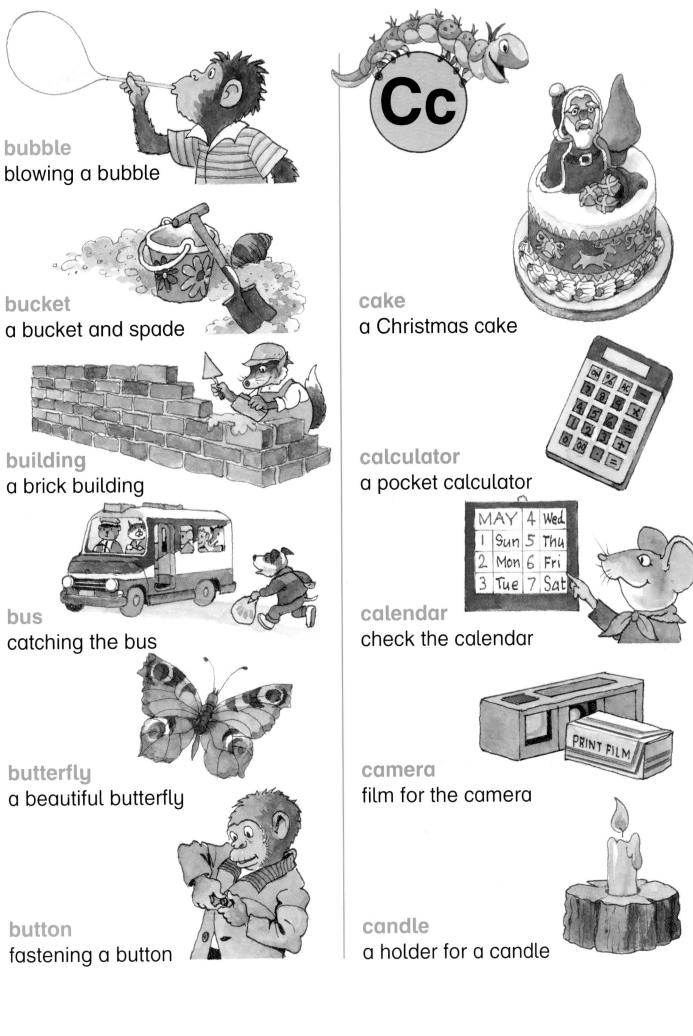

bubble
blowing a bubble

bucket
a bucket and spade

building
a brick building

bus
catching the bus

butterfly
a beautiful butterfly

button
fastening a button

Cc

cake
a Christmas cake

calculator
a pocket calculator

calendar
check the calendar

camera
film for the camera

candle
a holder for a candle

canoe
paddling a canoe

car
a sports car

caravan
a touring caravan

carrying
carrying a baby

castle
a haunted castle

cat
a cat with her kittens

caterpillar
a crawling caterpillar

cave
a pirate's cave

chair
a broken chair

chalk
drawing with chalk

cheese
a Swiss cheese

chicken
a chicken pecking corn

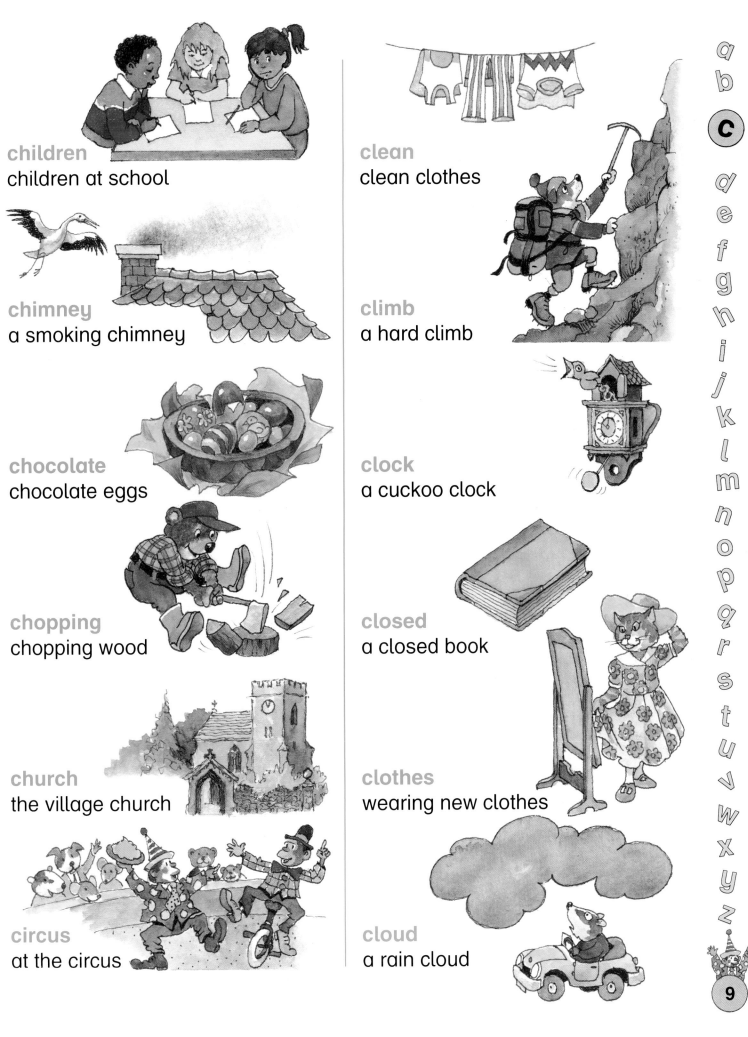

children
children at school

chimney
a smoking chimney

chocolate
chocolate eggs

chopping
chopping wood

church
the village church

circus
at the circus

clean
clean clothes

climb
a hard climb

clock
a cuckoo clock

closed
a closed book

clothes
wearing new clothes

cloud
a rain cloud

a b **c** d e f g h i j k l m n o p q r s t u v w x y z

9

clown
a cheeky clown

cold
shivering with cold

come
Come in!

comic
reading a comic

compact disc
playing a compact disc

computer
working with the computer

cooking
cooking the dinner

cottage
a cottage in the country

crane
towing with a crane

crayon
colouring with a crayon

crocodile
a crocodile swimming

crossing
crossing with care

crying
a crocodile crying

cupboard
an empty cupboard

cutting
cutting his hair

Dd

daffodil
a bunch of daffodils

daisy
daisy chains

dance
enjoying the dance

dangerous
a dangerous path

dark
a dark night

date
write the date

day
a windy day

dead
a dead wasp

dear
Dear Santa

deep
deep beneath the sea

dentist
needing a dentist

design
a toy design

desk
a writing desk

detective
a detective looking for fingerprints

diamond
a diamond ring

diary
our nature diary

dice
throwing the dice

different
different patterns

dig
dig the garden

digger
a digger making a hole

dinner
my favourite dinner

dinosaur
a meat-eating dinosaur

dirty
dirty shoes

disco
at the disco

dive
a graceful dive

doctor
a visit from the doctor

dog
a dog barking

doll
a rag doll

door
the front door

dragon
a Chinese dragon

drawing
drawing a picture

dream
a bad dream

a b c **d** e f g h i j k l m n o p q r s t u v w x y z

13

a b c **d e** f g h i j k l m n o p q r s t u v w x y z

dress
a fancy dress

drinking
drinking milk

driver
a bus driver

dropping
dropping the ball

drum
a big drum

duck
a duck with her ducklings

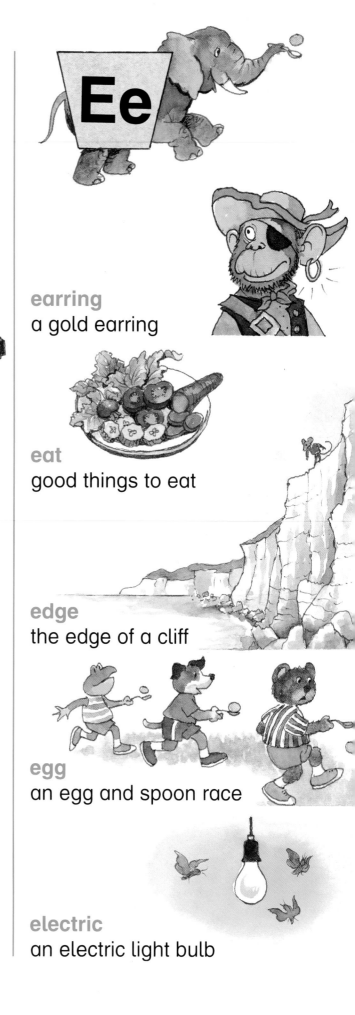

Ee

earring
a gold earring

eat
good things to eat

edge
the edge of a cliff

egg
an egg and spoon race

electric
an electric light bulb

elephant
an African elephant

embroidery
a piece of embroidery

empty
an empty box

end
the end of the story

engine
a car engine

entrance
pay at the entrance

envelope
opening the envelope

equal
equal length

even
even numbers

exercising
exercising on my bike

exit
leave by the exit

experiment
a scientific experiment

a b c d e f g h i j k l m n o p q r s t u v w x y z

explorer
an explorer at the North Pole

explosion
a loud explosion

eye
an eye patch

Ff

face
a happy face

fair
at the fair

falling
falling down a hole

farm
on the farm

farmer
a farmer at work

favourite
a favourite book

feather
a peacock feather

DO NOT FEED THE ANIMALS

feed
Do not feed the animals

field
a field of corn

find
find a fossil

finger
a finger puppet

finish
finish first

fire
a house on fire

fire-engine
a speeding fire-engine

fire-fighter
a fire-fighter at work

fireworks
a box of fireworks

fish
tropical fish

flag
waving a flag

floor
mopping the floor

flour
a bag of flour

a b c d e **f** g h i j k l m n o p q r s t u v w x y z

17

flower
a summer flower

flute
playing the flute

fly
a fly in my soup

fog
fog on the road

food
rabbit food

football
kicking a football

forest
a pine forest

fork
a knife and fork

fountain
a water fountain

fox
a hungry fox

fridge
a fridge full of food

friend
my best friend

18

frightened
a frightened horse

front
the front page

frost
frost on the window

fruit
a fruit tree

funny
a funny hat

fur
a kitten with soft fur

Gg

game
a game of dominoes

garage
in the garage

garden
a vegetable garden

gate
a wooden gate

gerbil
a gerbil nesting

a b c d e **f** **g** h i j k l m n o p q r s t u v w x y z

ghost
a scary ghost

giraffe
a giraffe feeding

girl
a little girl

give
give a kiss

glass
a glass of orange juice

glasses
sun glasses

glove
a lost glove

glue
stick with glue

goal
score a goal

gold
gold in a treasure chest

goldfish
a goldfish swimming

goodbye
waving goodbye

grass
lying in the grass

ground
bumpy ground

group
a pop group

growing
growing a sunflower

guinea-pig
a guinea-pig eating

guitar
playing a guitar

Hh

hair
curly hair

half
half past two

hear
hear the bells

heart
shape of a heart

hedgehog
a prickly hedgehog

helicopter
a helicopter flying

hello
saying hello

help
in need of help

hide
hide-and-seek

hill
a house on the hill

hippopotamus
a hippopotamus in mud

hold
hold my hand

hole
digging a hole

holiday
a seaside holiday

home
going home

honey
a pot of honey

horse
a horse in a stable

hospital
staying in hospital

house
a doll's house

hurt
a hurt knee

Ii

ice
sliding on ice

icicles
icicles hanging

ill
feeling ill

insect
an insect at work

instruments
musical instruments

invitation
a wedding invitation

iron
iron your shirt

island
a desert island

a b c d e f g h i j k l m n o p q r s t u v w x y z

23

Jj

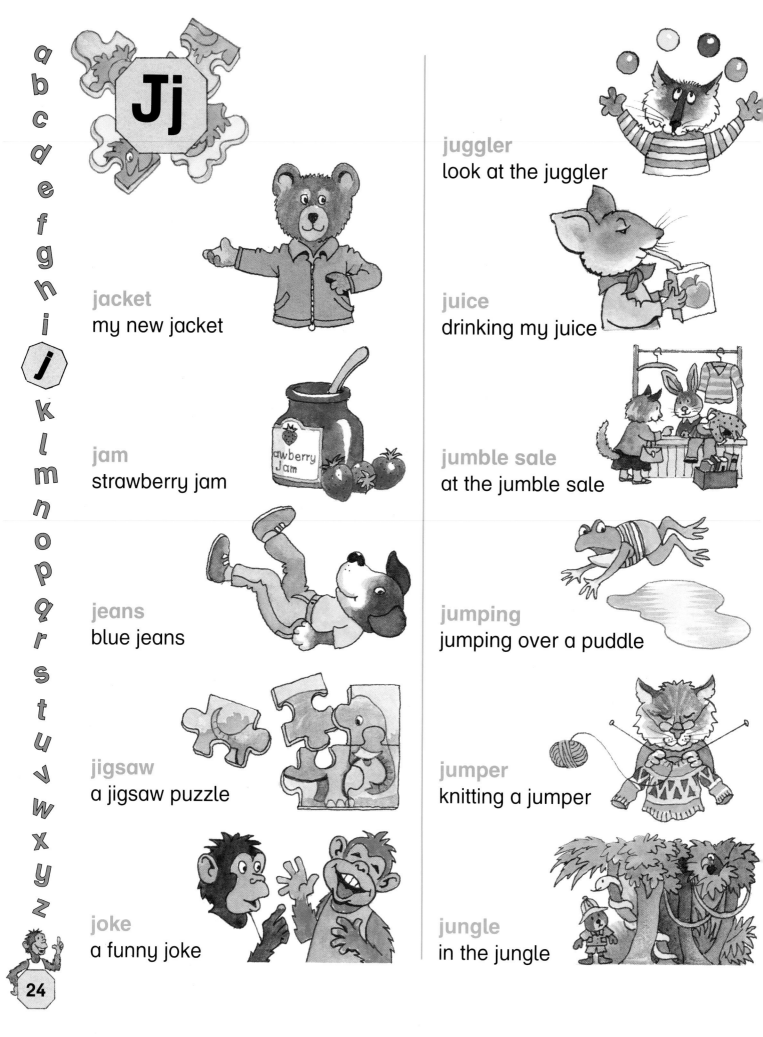

jacket
my new jacket

jam
strawberry jam

jeans
blue jeans

jigsaw
a jigsaw puzzle

joke
a funny joke

juggler
look at the juggler

juice
drinking my juice

jumble sale
at the jumble sale

jumping
jumping over a puddle

jumper
knitting a jumper

jungle
in the jungle

24

Kk

kangaroo
a kangaroo and her baby

kettle
a kettle boiling

key
keys on a key ring

kick
kick a stone

kitchen
cooking in the kitchen

kite
a kite in the sky

kitten
a kitten playing

knot
tying a knot

Ll

ladder
carrying a ladder

lady
an old lady

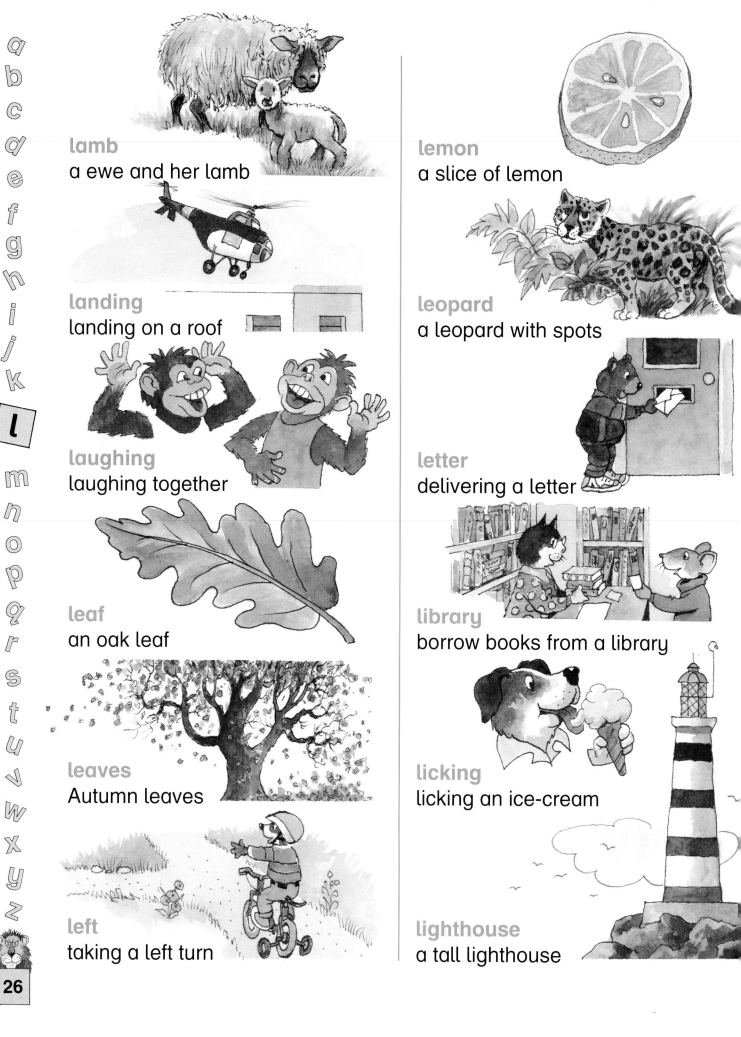

lamb
a ewe and her lamb

landing
landing on a roof

laughing
laughing together

leaf
an oak leaf

leaves
Autumn leaves

left
taking a left turn

lemon
a slice of lemon

leopard
a leopard with spots

letter
delivering a letter

library
borrow books from a library

licking
licking an ice-cream

lighthouse
a tall lighthouse

lightning
a flash of lightning

lion
a lion hunting

listen
listen to a tape

live
live in the 25th century

lorry
a dustbin lorry

lost
a lost teddy bear

love
Love from Grandad

Mm

machine
a washing machine

make
make a model

man
an old man

map
a treasure map

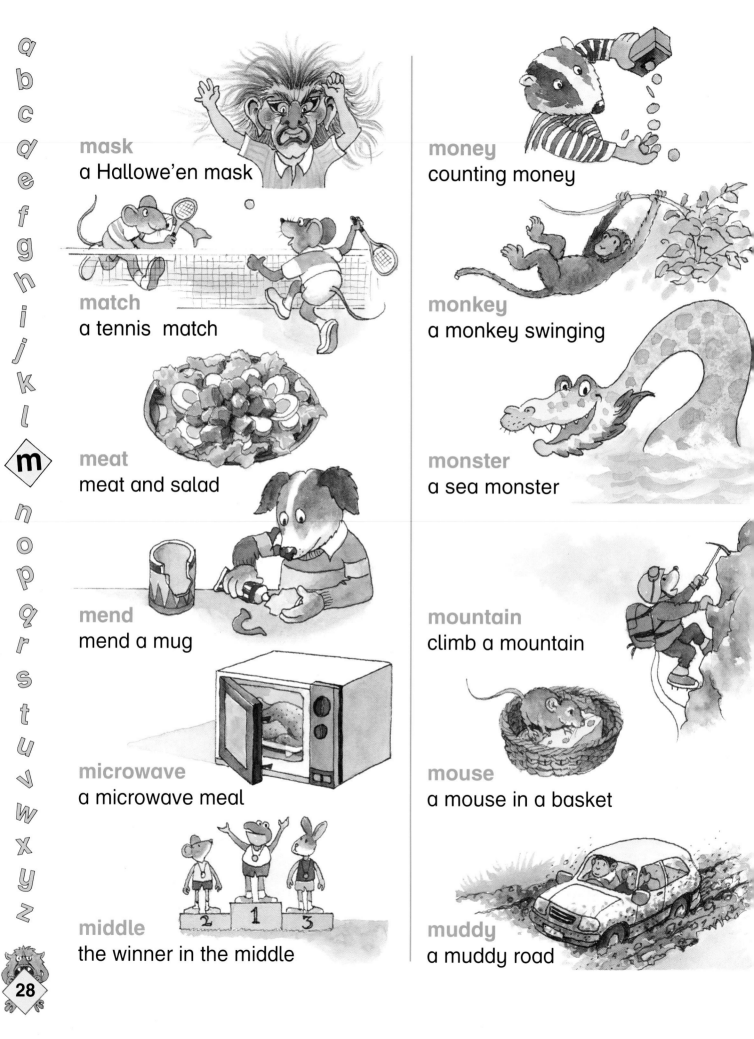

a b c d e f g h i j k l **m** n o p q r s t u v w x y z

mask
a Hallowe'en mask

match
a tennis match

meat
meat and salad

mend
mend a mug

microwave
a microwave meal

middle
the winner in the middle

money
counting money

monkey
a monkey swinging

monster
a sea monster

mountain
climb a mountain

mouse
a mouse in a basket

muddy
a muddy road

museum
an Egyptian museum

music
making music

Nn

name
writing my name

narrow
a narrow bridge

nature
the nature trail

naughty
a naughty puppy

necklace
a bead necklace

neighbour
our next door neighbour

nest
eggs in a nest

new
new at school

newspaper
reading the newspaper

a b c d e f g h i j k l **m** **n** o p q r s t u v w x y z

newt
a newt in the pond

nice
a nice day

night
night time

nightie
wearing my nightie

noise
a loud noise

notebook
writing in my notebook

notice
a notice board

nurse
a nurse at the clinic

nursery
in the nursery

Oo

ocean
a liner on the ocean

o'clock
two o'clock

octopus
an octopus with eight legs

odd
odd numbers

office
working in an office

oil
cooking oil

onion
slicing an onion

open
an open window

orange
peeling an orange

orchestra
playing in the orchestra

out
Keep Out!

oven
a cake in the oven

over
over the river

owl
an owl at night

a b c d e f g h i j k l m n **o** p q r s t u v w x y z

Pp

paint
a pot of paint

pair
a pair of cards

paper
folded paper dolls

parachute
a parachute jump

parcel
wrapping a parcel

Hello! Hello!

parrot
a talking parrot

party
dress for a party

pear
a juicy pear

peas
peas in a pod

pencil
sharpen a pencil

penguin
a penguin walking

people
a crowd of people

phone
making a phone call

photograph
taking a photograph

picture
a picture of me

pillow
a feather pillow

pilot
an airline pilot

pirate
a pirate ship

plane
a plane landing

plant
a house plant

plate
a plate of cakes

play
play the piano

police
a police car

a b c d e f g h i j k l m n o **p** q r s t u v w x y z

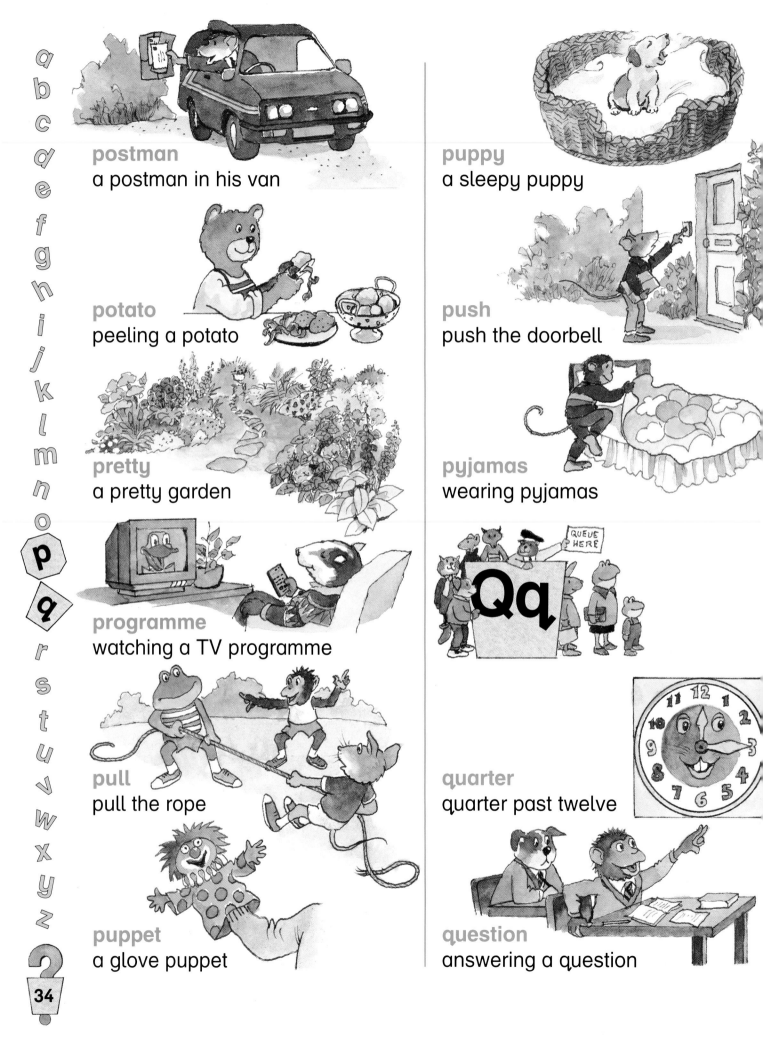

a b c d e f g h i j k l m n o **p** **q** r s t u v w x y z

postman
a postman in his van

potato
peeling a potato

pretty
a pretty garden

programme
watching a TV programme

pull
pull the rope

puppet
a glove puppet

puppy
a sleepy puppy

push
push the doorbell

pyjamas
wearing pyjamas

QUEUE HERE

Qq

quarter
quarter past twelve

question
answering a question

queue
Queue here

quick
a quick getaway

quiet
Quiet please!

quiz
a quiz show

Rr

rabbit
a white rabbit

race
the boat race

radio
listening to the radio

rain
heavy rain

rainbow
a rainbow after rain

read
learning to read

ready
ready, steady, go

a b c d e f g h i j k l m n o p **q r** s t u v w x y z

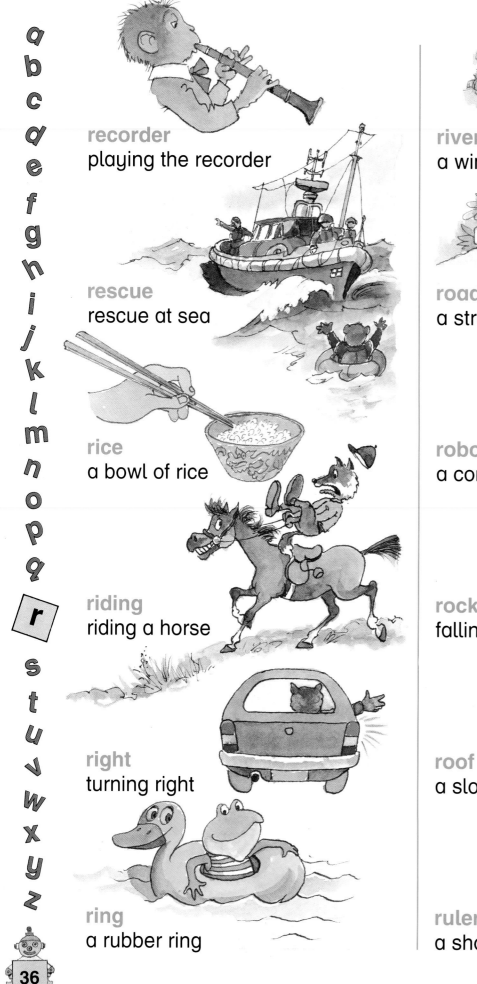

recorder
playing the recorder

rescue
rescue at sea

rice
a bowl of rice

riding
riding a horse

right
turning right

ring
a rubber ring

river
a winding river

road
a straight road

robot
a computer robot

rocks
falling rocks

roof
a sloping roof

ruler
a short ruler

Ss

sad
a sad face

sail
a sail board

sailor
a sailor on a boat

same
the same clothes

sand
covered with sand

sandwich
a thick sandwich

satellite
a satellite dish

scarf
a striped scarf

scary
a scary house

school
going to school

scissors
safe scissors

sea
a choppy sea

seaside
at the seaside

see
Can you see me?

seed
growing a seed

shadow
chasing my shadow

shallow
a shallow pool

shark
a hungry shark

sheep
a flock of sheep

shell
a sea shell

ship
a sailing ship

shoe
a ballet shoe

singing
a bird singing

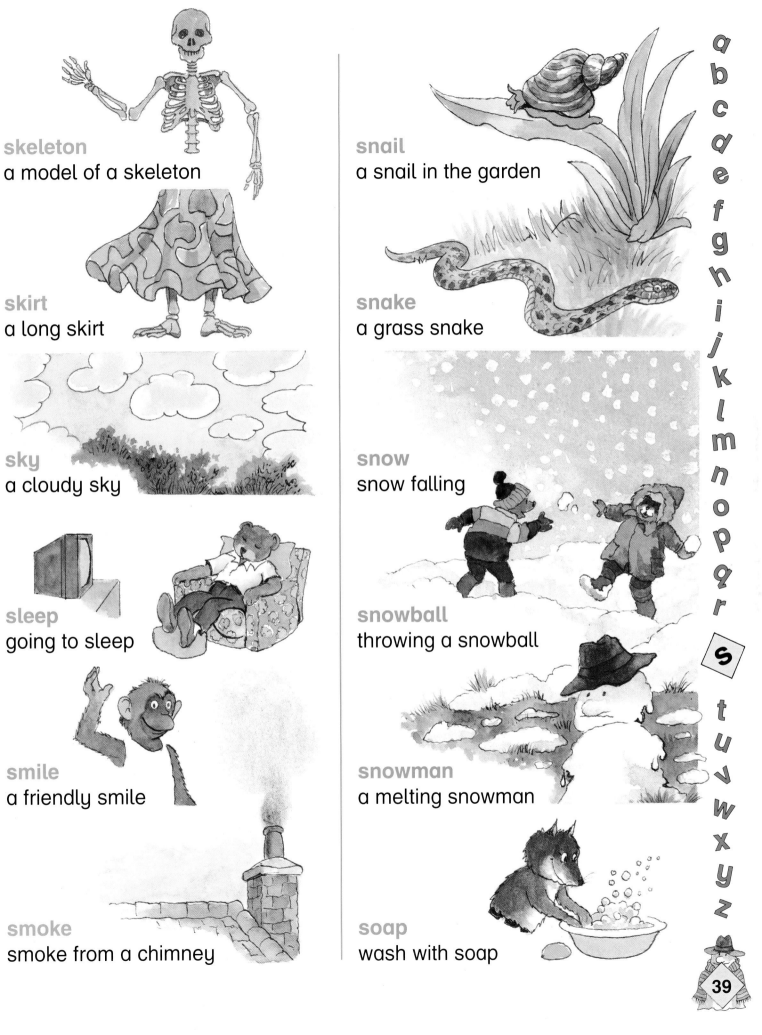

skeleton
a model of a skeleton

skirt
a long skirt

sky
a cloudy sky

sleep
going to sleep

smile
a friendly smile

smoke
smoke from a chimney

snail
a snail in the garden

snake
a grass snake

snow
snow falling

snowball
throwing a snowball

snowman
a melting snowman

soap
wash with soap

a b c d e f g h i j k l m n o p q r **s** t u v w x y z

sock
a hole in my sock

spaghetti
spaghetti with sauce

speak
speak French

spider
a spider in a web

spoon
a spoon for a baby

squirrel
a grey squirrel

staircase
a spiral staircase

stamp
a postage stamp

star
a gold star

start
start the car

station
the railway station

stay
stay in bed

stop
Stop! Children

story
reading a story

suitcase
pack a suitcase

supermarket
a supermarket trolley

supper
a drink for supper

sweets
selling sweets

Tt

table
the kitchen table

tadpole
a tadpole growing legs

tail
a very long tail

talk
having a serious talk

tape
a cassette tape

tea
a dolls' tea party

teacher
my favourite teacher

teeth
clean your teeth

telephone
choosing a telephone

television
repairing a television

tell
tell me a story

tent
camping in a tent

thank you
saying *thank you*

throwing
throwing a stick

thunder
thunder and lightning

tiger
a tiger in the jungle

time
tell the time

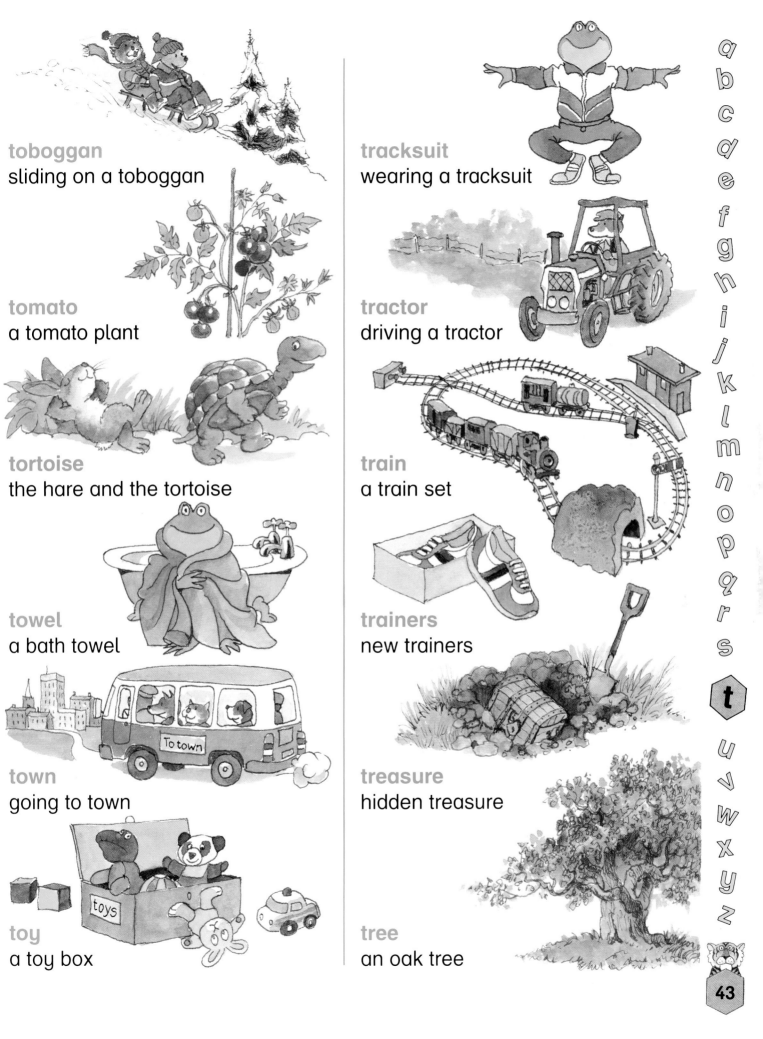

toboggan
sliding on a toboggan

tomato
a tomato plant

tortoise
the hare and the tortoise

towel
a bath towel

town
going to town

toy
a toy box

tracksuit
wearing a tracksuit

tractor
driving a tractor

train
a train set

trainers
new trainers

treasure
hidden treasure

tree
an oak tree

a b c d e f g h i j k l m n o p q r s **t** u v w x y z

43

trousers
long trousers

trumpet
blowing a trumpet

tunnel
a railway tunnel

typewriter
keys on a typewriter

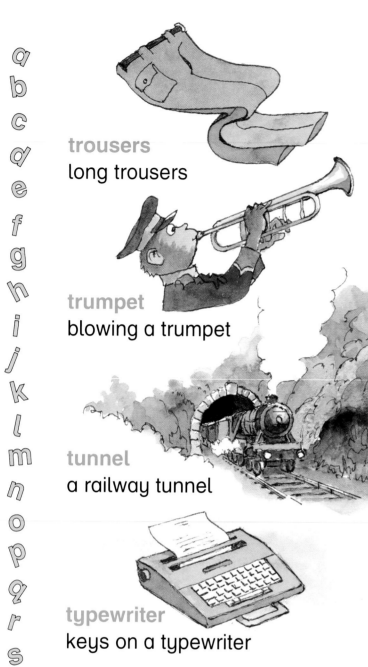

Uu

ugly
an ugly duckling

umbrella
a striped umbrella

under
under the table

uniform
a school uniform

untidy
untidy clothes

upset
feeling upset

upside down
hanging upside down

Vv

video
a video camera

vacuum cleaner
using a vacuum cleaner

view
a view of the sea

valentine
a valentine card

village
a small village

valley
flowers in the valley

violin
a violin and bow

vase
a vase of flowers

visit
a visit to the park

vegetables
fresh vegetables

volcano
a volcano erupting

Ww

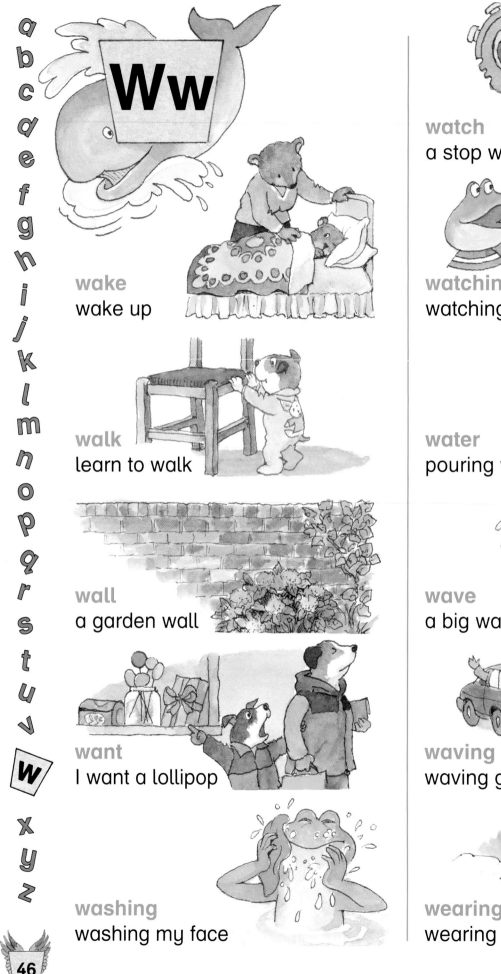

wake
wake up

walk
learn to walk

wall
a garden wall

want
I want a lollipop

washing
washing my face

watch
a stop watch

watching
watching a clown

water
pouring water

wave
a big wave

waving
waving goodbye

wearing
wearing warm clothes

weather
bad weather

wedding
at a wedding

weekend
enjoying the weekend

weigh
weigh yourself

whale
a whale blowing

wheel
a steering wheel

wheelbarrow
pushing a wheelbarrow

whistle
blowing a whistle

wild
wild animals

windmill
the sails on a windmill

window
a window box

wing
a bird's wing

woman
a young woman

woods
walk in the woods

working
working in the garden

world
a globe of the world

worm
a worm in an apple

write
write a letter

Xx

X-ray
looking at an X-ray

xylophone
playing the xylophone

Yy

yacht
a yacht in the harbour

yawn
give a big yawn

year
a one-year-old baby

yellow
a yellow dress

yoghurt
eating a yoghurt

yolk
egg yolk

young
a young chick

yo-yo
playing with a yo-yo

Zz

zebra
a striped zebra

zigzag
a zigzag line

zip
fastening a zip

zoo
at the zoo

zooming
zooming into space

a b c d e f g h i j k l m n o p q r s t u v w x y z

Words we write a lot

a	end	into	played	they
about	every	is	playing	things
after	everyone	it	please	this
again		like	pulled	to
all	family	little	pushed	too
am	for	look		
an	from	looking	quickly	under
and			quietly	up
are	get	made		upon
as	getting	make	reading	us
at	go	making	run	
away	goes	me	running	very
	going	more		
back	good	my	said	wanted
be	got	myself	saw	was
because	great		see	we
big		naughty	she	went
but	had	new	sit	were
by	has	nice	sitting	what
	have	no	some	when
called	having	not	speaking	where
came	he		story	who
can	her	of		with
can't	here	off	talking	
come	him	old	telling	you
comes	home	on	thank	your
coming	house	once	that	
		only	the	
did	I	or	their	
do	if	other	them	
doing	in	our	then	
down	inside	out	there	

Numbers

 0 zero
nought

 1 one

 2 two

 3 three

 4 four

 5 five

 6 six

 7 seven

 8 eight

 9 nine

 10 ten

11 eleven
12 twelve
13 thirteen
14 fourteen
15 fifteen
16 sixteen
17 seventeen
18 eighteen
19 nineteen
20 twenty
30 thirty
40 forty
50 fifty
60 sixty
70 seventy
80 eighty
90 ninety
100 one hundred

1st first
2nd second
3rd third
4th fourth
5th fifth
6th sixth
7th seventh
8th eighth
9th ninth
10th tenth

Words we use in maths

big

small

slow

fast

long

short

thick

thin

narrow   wide

high

low

empty   full

first   last

tall   small

light

heavy

more   less

whole

part

52

The calendar

autumn

winter

summer

spring

Months of the year

December

November   January

October   February

September   March

August   April

July   May

June

Days of the week

Sunday

Saturday   Monday

Friday   Tuesday

Thursday   Wednesday

53

A visit to the clinic

waiting-room

scales

measuring   weighing

eye-testing chart

A
stxbue
rmhoynkl
cfjzpqdgn
acsuwgbiu

optician

---

the human body

head
shoulder
elbow
hip
hand
leg
foot

hair
ear
eye
nose
mouth

wrist
knee
toes

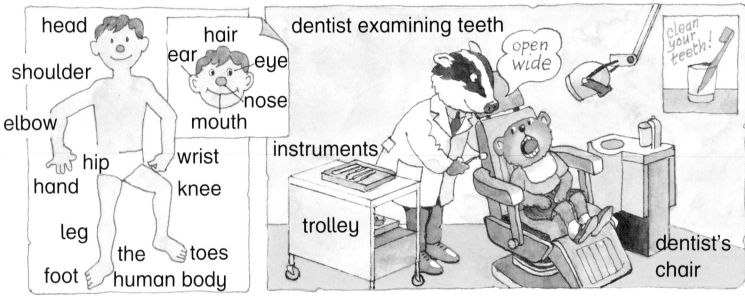

dentist examining teeth

open wide

Clean your teeth!

instruments

trolley

dentist's chair

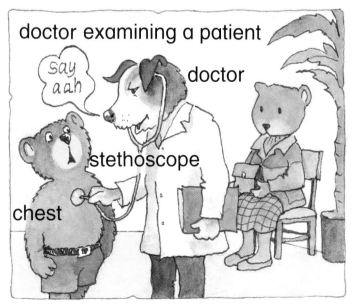

doctor examining a patient

say aah

doctor

stethoscope

chest

nurse

x-ray

patient

broken bone
bandages

leg in plaster

medicine

A picnic in the park

kite

dad

mum

jogger

little brother

uncle

grandma

sister

hamper

birthday cake

cousins

cards

presents

knife

crisps

sandwiches

orange drinks

paper plates

grandad

friend

toddler

aunt

Our classroom

mobiles

paint pots

sink

flowers

water tray

counting

the teacher

maths table

technology table

models

easel

brush

overall

trays

painting a picture

plant

ome
and
ead

reading

listening

building with bricks

earphones

story tape

mirror

clothes box

dressing up

57

At the playground

bench

swings

tyres

mum

baby

pushing the swing

buggy

bucket and spade

sand castle

digging in the sandpit

roundabout

climbir frame

sand pies

Ice Cream

queui

sitting on the fence

see-saw

slide

sliding down

climbing net

splashing in
the pool

gate

59

Sports Day

running a race

catching

doing gymnastics

slide

lifeguard

chasing

throwing

skipping with ropes

to the pool

swimming

diving-board

a game of football

60

Outer space

asteroids

planets

satellite

rocket

moon

Earth

spacecraft

space station

lifeline

spacesuit

space shuttle

astronaut

61

Once upon a time...

a wizard casting a spell

wand

wicked witch

the three billy goats gruff

trol[l]

Fairy Godmother

Tom Thumb

Prince Charming

Cinderella

the seven dwarfs

Puss in boots

gingerbrea[d] house

the Frog Prince

Hansel and Gretel

crown

a castle in the sky

Queen

Goldilocks

the three bears

giant

genie

Jack
and the
beanstalk

wolf

Aladdin's
lamp

Red
Riding Hood

...they all lived happily ever after.

Index